Dating from the 19th of June, two artificial ports were on site and set with great difficulties. They were composed of 6000 Tons Phoenix casings (caissons). From the 10th of July onwards the port of Arromanches will handle daily 6000 Tons of supplies.

As early as the 4th of July, the Navy could boast of having landed, one million men, 183.500 vehicles and 650.000 Tons of supplies. From then on the Germans had lost their local superiority in numbers and material.

ARROMANCHES 44
THE NORMANDY INVASION

TEXT : J. DE LAUNAY
PICTURES : J. DE SCHUTTER
TRANSLATION : MAJOR D. KELLY, Special Forces

EDITOR J.M. COLLET

The authors wish to express
their particular gratitude to
Dr. Jean-Pierre BENAMOU
President of the Association
of the Caen Museum 1944
for his advice and documentation.

D 1984/2070/45

The opponents:

Side of the Allies: Eisenhower (1) was supreme Commander assisted by General Montgomery (2)

German Side: Marshal Von Rundstedt (3) is assisted by Marshal Rommel (4)

Each time I think of that day, twenty years ago, I say to myself that I shall have to find means of oevring for peace in order that the world shall enjoy eternal peace.

I hope with all may soul that we shall never again see scenes similar to those of that Landing Day, twenty years ago. I pray that Humanity may have learned that great lesson.

D.D. Eisenhower, 6 June 1964.

4

PRELUDE

1. The "Overlord" decision

Since the Québec Conference *(Quadrant)* the Overlord Operation has top priority in Roosevelt and Churchill's preoccupations.

The Big Three meet, for the first time, in Theheran, from the 28th of November to the 1st of December 1943. The meeting had been prepared by a Conference of the Foreign Ministers, Hull, Eden, Molotov and the Chinaman Fou Ping-Scheng, held in Moscow from the 19th of October to the 1st of November. The Russians appeared courteous and accepted the Anglo-American proposal to create the United Nations Organisation without however wavering from the essential objective : the setting off of the Overlord operation. The Ministers agreed on subsidiary questions : l'*Anschluss* is considered null and void, Austria will retrieve its independance, the war criminels, a list of whom is established, will be brought and punished on the sites of their crimes; Turkey will be invited to enter war on the Allies side.

On their way to Teheran Churchill and Roosevelt stopped off at Cairo in order ro meet the Tchang Kaï-chek couple, as always engaged on their beneficial haggling (*Sextant* Conference).

The Teheran Conference (*Eureka*) took place in the Palace of the Soviet Ambassador, as security was very difficult to maintain. In this country occupied by English and Soviet troops, agitation, in fact, is great. The Soviets support the Iranian Communist Parti, *Toudeh*, established in 1942, and help it to obtain all key positions. The British, masters of the petrol industry, strengthen the anti-communist militias and encourage the nationalists in order to defend their own interests. The ones and the others imprison and deport all who oppose their hegemony, in particular 250 Iranian personalities, accused of *collaboration* with Germany. The Royal Dutch Shell struggles against British Petroleum. The English endeavour to distribute to their friends the proceeds of the U.S. Lease Rend until the arrival, in 1943, of an American Mission of ... 30.000 men who will from then on fight for the interests of the U.S. petroleum companies. The Iranians try to play one against the other in order to safeguard their independance.

It is, therefore, not astonishing that Himmler should also have tried to play his cards from the 22 to the 27th of November, German commandos were dropped in Iran, with mission to destroy the Three Big Powers. They were captured by the Soviet Police arriving in strength in Teheran.

Surrounded in a protected area by more than 5000 policemen Roosevelt, Churchill and Staline have talks in peace. Churchill caught a cold, suffors from his throat, but thanks to numerous inhalations he will succeed in saying all that had to be said.

Roosevelt in excellent physical condition shows great pleasure at meeting Staline for the first time. The President, bent on charming and

End of Mai 1944 in the course of the final inspection by Marshal Rommel (on his right General Marks).

Here is to be seen how the personnel of the Atlantic Wall mustered (festing Europa).

The Admiral Theodor Krancke is in command of the Naval Forces in the West (Marinegruppe West).

The art of camouflage.

This false villa hides a 105 mm canon.

This other villa integrated in the landscape is an observation post.

This is a command post.

on seducing his interlocutor succeeds with effort.

Since August 1943, Roosevelt is in possession of the forecasts of his military advisors.

The post-war situation of Russia, in Europe, will be predominant. Germany beaten, there will be no country in Europe, susceptible of counterbalancing her fantastic military potential.

The conclusion to be reached is the following : as in this war, Russia is the deciding factor, it is essential to give her the maximum possible assistance and every effort should be made to obtain her friendship. And, as without a doubt, she will dominate Europe, after the defeat of the Powers of the Axe, it is all the more essential to entertain and retain, in the future, the most friendly relations with her.

For the United States, the most important consideration with respect to Russia, is the pursuance of the war in the Pacific. If Russia becomes our ally against the Japanese, the war could end much sooner, and the losses in lives and material, could be much less. If Russia should decide on an unfriendly or negative policy the difficulties of the war in the Pacific would be much greater and the operations might even fail.

Churchill and Roosevelt arrived in Teheran without a concerted plan. The British Prime Minister as always, favours "*Overlord*" but wishes to put back its realisation until after Rome and Rhodes have been taken. The U.S. President, influenced by Marshall, is well decided to maintain the "*Overlord*" operation at the date decided upon by the military chiefs : 1st May 1944.

Upon his arrival, Roosevelt has a private interview with Staline. They find common subjects of preoccupation the second front should be opened in order to divert thirty to forty German divisions from the East front; the French are irritating gossipers, and Pétain, better than de Gaulle, expresses the inclinations of his *compatriotes*.

The uncommited countries (*Tiers-Monde*) should attain independance, whatever might be Churchill's opinion on India. Roosevelt makes friends with Staline by making fun of Churchill, he will remain true to this attitude during the complete conference, shunning private interviews with Churchill.

The conceptions however, differ, Churchill distrusts Staline's territorial ambitions, who in turn, mistrusts the British of wishing to intervene in the Balkans thus preceeding the Red Army. Roosevelt, obsessed by the operation Overlord and having realised in Europe the Soviet Fire Break is afraid that Churchill and Staline should agree in order to give priority to the Balkans action.

Staline counts the German divisions in action : eight in Jugoslavia, five in Greece, three in Bulgaria, twenty-five in France.

Churchill summarizes the conditions of success of Overlord :

To obtain mastery of the air in the West; reduce to twelve mobile divisions the German reserves in the same region; prevent, during the first sixty days, the arrival of fifteen divisions, diverted from other fronts.

It becomes therefore indispensable to pin down in Italy and

A quiet control post, and a liaison headquarters post.

New style baudy house.

This make believe cow herd in order to stop gliders. They are absolutely complete, with sharp tails.

Yugoslavia as much as possible of the enemy potential. In Italy there is no question of proceeding beyond the line Pise-Rimini. But, as thirty enemy divisions are held by the Yugoslav partisans, the Balkans appear to be the ideal region, to delay the arrival of enemy support :

The Balkanic theater was, assuredly, one of the regions where we could put the enemy in difficulty and make easier the hard battles with which we were faced. All we required was to pin to the ground those thirty enemy divisions. Messers, Molotov, Eden and one of the President's delegates could discuss the details and inform the conference on all the political aspects of the question. For example, did our friends and allies the Soviets see any political difficulty in the presented project. If so, which one ? We were determined to act in harmony with them. From a military stand point, it was out of question to foresee using important forces in this region. The object was solely to help the Partisans, by supplying material, supplies and by performing a few commando operations.

The crucial problem has come to light. Roosevelt referees according to Staline's and his own desires :

1. *The reunion of the three General staffs will take for granted that the operation "Overlord" will constitute the priority military target of 1944.*
2. *They will make suggestions concerning secondary operations to be carried out, endeavouring, by all possible means, not to delay the start of Overlord.*

This double recommendation is transmitted on the 30th of November, to the Military Committee. Roosevelt and Churchill promise Staline to set "D" Day in May 1944.

2. The high command of "Overlord" operation

In Cairo, Roosevelt and Churchill settled many other problems, the principal of which was, without contest, the designation of the commander in chief of Overlord.

Churchill and Brooke endeavour, once more, to interest Roosevelt in the idea of an attack on Rhodes — always the peripheric strategy — but the President is adamant in his firm position.

Even the villas are ringed and provided with crenels.

Here is a make belief aeroplane on a make-belief aerodrome.

In order to help Overlord, a secondary operation will take place in the South of France. The"Anvil" Landing, the idea of which originated in Québec and progressed in Teheran.

Churchill and Brooke therefore concentrate their efforts on the *Anvil* landing; all the more so, as on the 5th of December, Roosevelt gained a further point: the designation of an American commander in chief for Overlord, who is to be General Eisenhower and not Marshall, whom Roosevelt prefers to keep next to him in Washington, nor Brooke to whom previously Churchill had promised the post.

Eisenhower had brillianty succeeded in North Africa and Southern Italy. The hopes which Marshall had vested in this excellent staff officer were confirmed. Born in a modest Kansas family, this fine round headed athlete, with muscular neck, is the typical good pupil; sensible well educated and well behaved. He prepares at the same time the school of Annapolis, where he succeeds in obtaining first place, and the Military School of West Point, where he enters with number two. He chooses West Point and comes out sub-lieutenant in 1915. In charge of the instruction of the U.S. Expeditionary Corps, he afterwards obtains brillant diplomas at the Army War College (major out of 275 pupils) and at the Army Industrial College. From 1933 to 1935, he follows Mac Arthur to the Philippines as chief of General staff. The army chiefs consider him as a specialist in relations between the Army and the Navy and the Air Force, and as such in December 1941, General Marshall nominates him, at the age of fifty one, Assistant Chief of the Bureau of Combined Operations. His cordial gentleness, his good-natured authority, his capacity for work designated him for the command of the Allied Armies in North Africa where he succeeds in gaining the good will of all concerned: from Churchill to Roosevelt and from Marshall to Brooke. He showed unfailing patience towards the pretentious Frenchmen, Darlan and Juin, de Gaulle and Giraud, the muddling Italians Victor Emmanual and Sforza, Badoglio and Bonomi; the Marocains and the Tunisians. He succeeded in softening the asperities of Montgomery's character, he calmed the boiling Patton and disarmed the refrigerating King, remaining at the same time the disciplined executive of General Marshall. Everybody obeys him and he finally only knows one chief: Marshall.

It's in Cairo that Eisenhower learns of his nomination, the 7th of December 1943. He then pays two visits to Churchill: in Carthage where he finds him in bed with pneumonia, and Marrakech the 30th of December; he will then spend two weeks with Marshall in Washington. The 14th of January he settles down in London in his new appointment.

Eisenhower will be in command of the thirty five divisions of Overlord, fifteen English and Canadian divisions and twenty U.S. divisions. In the initial phase of the operation, the land forces will be under the command of Montgomery. The other assistants to the commander in chief will be, for the naval forces, Admiral Ramsay; for the Air Force,

Reality is obviously very different, here any visitor will be well received. ↑   *The battery of cap de la Heve at the North of the Seine estuary.* ↓

This tower of a Renault Tank FT 17 has taken roots.   This canon is protected by a shelter.

Marshal Leigh-Mallory, both English. His chief of staff will be the U.S. general Bedell Smith. At supreme level he is assisted by Air Marshal Tedder (British) his eventual successor.

Eisenhower's task is diplomatic and logistic : to amortize all clashes at all levels, to bring at the times and dates fixed in advance, the foreseen means in men and material. Ike will be the station master of a huge marshalling yard.

He used to say :
— *I am not a real General but the Boss of a huge enterprise.*

It will be his responsability to ship to Europe several million men : 185.000 of whom on D-Day and a million and a half in the course of the six following weeks, to unload 12.000 Tons of material per day. Indeed the planning was already prepared by the chief of staff of the Supreme Allied Command (COSSAC) F. Morgan but as Eisenhower reported to Marshal :

— *The sites of the various headquarters, the exact communicating system, the strength of the units, the quantity of material, in short no question was properly solved.*

Ike undertakes, with luck, the task, during four months, in order to be ready, on D Day the 1st of May 1944. To help him he disposes of a combined staff (SHAEF), which will go from 1000 persons in January 1944 to 5.000 in July and 16.000 one year later in conformity with the application of the galloping law of Parkinson.

The (COSSAC) plan which Churchill had instigated i.e. one hundred and thirteen pages of official paper and ten explanatory maps, insist on the preliminary conditions of success :
— *mastery of the seas*
— *mastery of the air*
— *Less than twelve ennemy mobile divisions in North West Europe*
— *prevent the ennemy from bringing to the theater of operations fifteen reserve divisions during 2 months.*

The document mentions various secondary incidents, but not negligeable : the tides, the moon, the wind.

Furthermore, Eisenhower knows, as the English have repeatedly reminded him of the fact, that never until the Second World War has an amphibious landing succeeded.

3. Mastery of the seas

In the course of the Year 1943, the Allies reversed the situation in the Atlantic since the 30th of January 1943, Admiral Doenitz head of the German submarines has replaced grand admiral Raeder at the command of the German fleet.

All this has meant considerable work by the German "Todt" Organisation.

The Atlantic Wall

This defense was built as from the 23^d of March 1942, the most important work starting beginning of the autumn of 1942.

From Frieseland to the Bidassoa were foressen some 15.000 defense sites, two thirds of which between the Escaut and the Loire rivers. They were to be divided into 4.000 main sites and 10.000 small blockhouses. All defended by 500.000 men.

In May 1943, 6.000 sites had been completed. In July 8.000. Nominated in November 1943 inspector of the coast fortifications, Rommel will increase their efficiency by placing on the beaches 800 traps or obstacles to the kilometer. Unlike Rundstedt, Rommel believed in the invulnerability of the wall.

Furthermore all the ports were organised in autonomous fortresses in order to consolidate the entirety and hinder the landings which could reach a certain level only in the ports.

In the landing zone, over 500 kms, 1.643 sites were completed (out of the 2.011 foreseen) that is to say 4 sites per km, and equipped with 4.000 cannons.

Immediately at the rear of the zone, 2 million mines and 300.000 stakes covered the surrounding country.

The "Todt" organisation employed for this colossal task 291.000 people, 15.000 of which were Germans, 85.000 French, and 191.000 Foreigners. Amongst these Foreigners, in numerical order, Russians, Poles, Italians and Spanish Republicans.

Allied Organigram

Commander in chief General Eisenhower : assistant Tedder			
Combined staff			
Navy Adm. Ramsay	21 army group BR General Montgomery	12st army group US General Bradley	Air Forces General Leigh-Mallory

German Organigram

Oberbefehlshaber West (OB West) Commander in chief West from Antwerp to Monaco Mal von Rundstedt - St Germain en Laye			
B army group from Antwerp to Nantes Mal Rommel - La Roche Guyon		G army group from Nantes to Monaco General Blaskowitz-Rouffiac	
7th army Nantes-Houlgate General Dollmann-Le Mans	15th army Houlgate-Antwerp General von Salmuth-Tourcoing	1st army Atlantic	19th army Mediterraneen

According to the will of Rommel, the assailant should be expected from the Beaches.↓
The undermentioned should block the tanks.   ↓

These "asparagus type obstacles" are capped by a mine or a trapped shell these Tchecoslovakian "porcupines" were foreseen to prevent any deployment of troops.

1. The German forces on the Western front - 6 June 1944

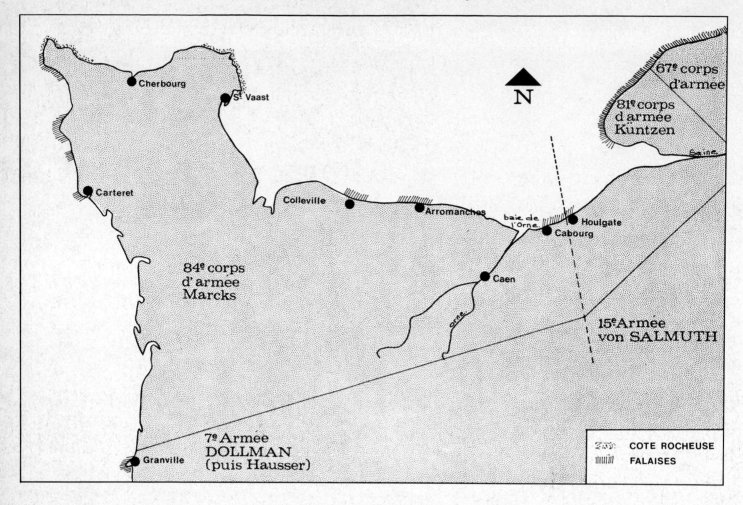

2. The allied landing forces - 6 June 1944

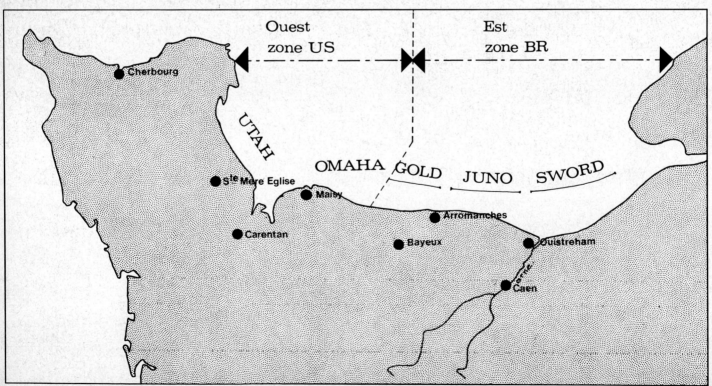

The ground is mined ← These rails await the tanks.
→ These porcupines protect the complete length of the
coast. ↓ ↓
These obstacles are ready to stop the landing craft. ↓ ↓ ↓

D-Day : Reaction of the german coast batteries

Out of the 28 German coast batteries in working order only 11 fired on the assaulting forces : La Pernelle II (3 x 170). Saint-Marcouf (3 x 210). Azeville (4 x 105). Maisy I (4 x 100). Maisy II (6 x 155). Longues (4 x 152). Ver sur Mer. La Mare (4 x 105). Ver sur Mer. Fleury (4 x 122). Houlgate (6 x 155). Mont Canisy (6 xc 155). Le Havre-Bléville (3 x 170). 5 were immediately put out of action : Morsalines (6 x 155). Bény (4 x 100). Colleville (4 x 105). Ouistreham (4 x 105). Riva Bella (6 x 155). The other 12 were incapable of firing one shot.

In spite of these partial setbacks, one can consider that the landing area batteries and those of the Cherbourg area fully performed their task. The German downfall was not due to this side, but to the loss of mastery of the air and the slow reaction of Hitler in sending the 12th and 21st armoured divisions and the Panzer Lehr to the fighting area.

Much could be said about the quality of the troops manning the defenses. Young and insufficiently trained. ↑
Cosacs not adapted to the climate ←
Various slav. elements → → or territorials →

The Air Force reconnaissance is doing wonders. From the 1st of April to the 5th of June 1944, in the course of 4.500 raids, they photograph all the beaches and coastal defenses from Biarritz to Rotterdam. The efficiency of their work is of a quality never attained to-date.

Let us add that this task was completed by reports and the stealing of enemy plans, carried out by the French Resistance and by reconnaissance missions carried out by the Commandos and the Navy.

The other missions were the responsability of the strategical and tactical Air Forces. They dispose of four months to effect their task, but the problems of the command and the targets have not yet been settled. The chiefs of stragetical Air Force, General Spaatz (*U.S. Stragetical Air Force*) and Marshal Harris (*Royal Air Force*) are not at all convinced of the necessity for *Overlord*. They feel that the enemy could be brought to mercy, by their sole bombing. Spying and reconnaissance flights have on the other hand established, as from 1943, that Germany is preparing a secret weapon; the rockets, which might change the factors of war in the air.

The 17th of August 1943, Harris launched 597 bombers on the base of Peenemünde. The Germans were obliged to transfer their fabrications to the underground factories of the Harz mountains and their testing Center to Poland. Now, in the beginning of 1944, the reconnaissance flights and spying help to discover more or less twenty launching ramps in the Somme, the North and Pas de Calais Areas. It is therefore clear that the use of rockets has only been delayed. According to Spaatz and Harris the Air war is only at its beginning.

Eisenhower does not agree with this point of view. According to him, dating form D. Day-90 all the armed forces must be put under his command the Navy as well as the Strategical Air Force.

— *Otherwise, all I have to do is to return home, he declares to Churchill on the 3d of March.*

— *If this question is not setted immediately, I shall ask to be relieved of my command, he advises the Pentagone on the 22nd of March.*

The 26th of March Eisenhower obtains satisfaction, all the strategic Air Force based in Britain and Southern Italy is placed under his command. His assistant, Marshal Tedder will be responsible for liaison.

This problem solved, Eisenhower is confronted in March and April with another dilemma :

— *General Spaatz backed by Harris has laid out an « Oil Plan » the object of which is to destroy the factories and fuel reserves.*
— *Marshal Tedder preconises a transportation plan the target of which is to dislocate the Ennemy Communications.*

Both targets are carried out simultaneously, but the second task will be the responsability of the Tactical Air Force (*U.S. Force and 2nd Tactical Royal Air Force*) under the command of Leigh-Mallory.

We have mentioned further on the effects of strategic bombardments, but we should like to note, as from this moment that the Oil Plan of Spaatz-Harris launched by *Ike* the 19th of April was well imagined. The object was to destroy the synthetic fuel manufacturing plants which Germany had the greatest need for. From January to May 1944, the strategic Air Force only succeeds in reducing German production by 2.5 %, percentage insufficient to reduce consumption. It is only on the 28th and 29th of May that strategic Air Command achieves a raid of 1576 bombers ont Pölitz in Pomerania and hits very heavily the enemy.

The petrol problem (aviation fuel)
- in thousands of tons -

1944	Needed	Production	Consumption
Januar	165	159	122
Februar	165	164	135
March	169	181	156
April	172	175	164
May	184	156	195

In June the production drop was 75 %.

The Allies will win the Petrol battle only in June, after the conquest by the Roumanians, of the Petrol Wells of Ploesti. From then on Germany will be able to dispose of only 10 to 20 % of her needs.

1944	Needs	Production	Consumption
June	198	52	182
July	207	35	136
August	213	17	115
September	221	10	60
October	228	20	53
November	230	49	53
December	223	26	44

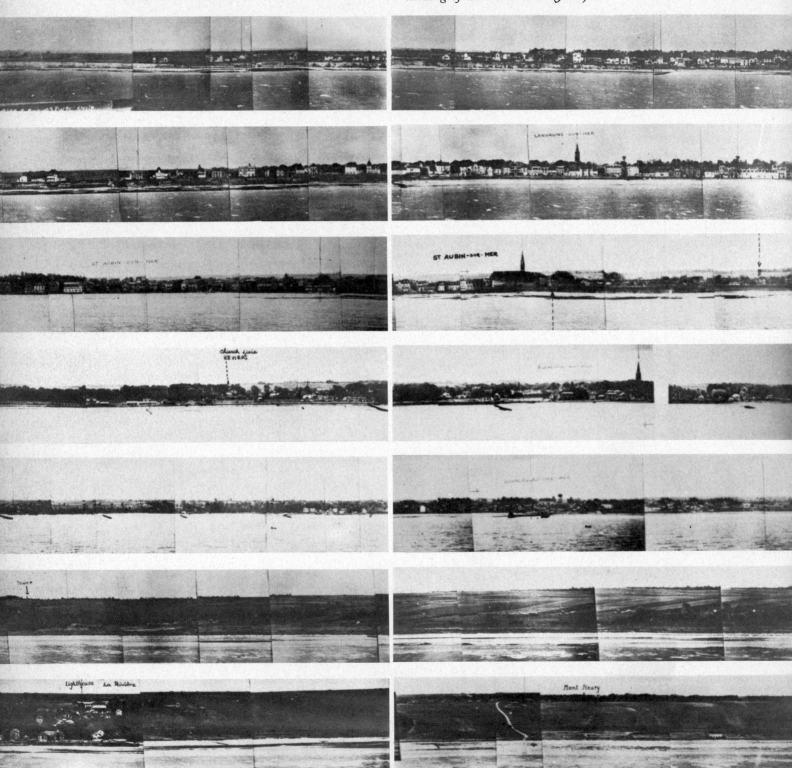

In March 1944, the admiralty had photographed by sub-marine the complete landing coast. Only the territory foreseen for the landing of British Forces (Juno).

26

In March 1944 the French resistance supplied the nature of the obstacles, but still a number of unknown factors subsist. For exemple the quality of the ground (clay, mud or sand) is revealed neither by these photos nor by the air reconnaissance.

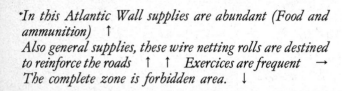

In this Atlantic Wall supplies are abundant (Food and ammunition) ↑
Also general supplies, these wire netting rolls are destined to reinforce the roads ↑ ↑ *Exercices are frequent* →
The complete zone is forbidden area. ↓

By the end of 1944, the deficit in Aviation Fuel is more than 400.000 Tons : the *Luftwaffe* is from then on condemned.

It remains however that on D-Day the petrol production had not been seriously impaired by Strategic Air Force.

We will also ascertain that the bombing of the War manufacturing plants did not prevent Germany from reaching its peak production outputs during the first 6 months of 1944.

One could therefore question whether such raids, some of which required several million liters of fuel, do not represent a great wastage of means, which might have prolonged the War.

The mission of the Tactical Air Force presents other problems. Its target is to destroy the enemy communications lines, to prevent the eventual arrival of reserves and to isolate for D.Day all the Landing Area.

A report by Professor Zuckerman, an operational research man, made a choice of 72 Targets = 39 in Germany, 33 in France and Belgium which must be reached in order to attain this project between D.Day-90 and D.Day.

Spaatz and Harris are of the opinion that these targets — Marshalling yards, locomotives, signal boxes, shunting points are difficult to pin point and easy to repair when damaged. Tedder, however maintains his point of view.

Furthermore, this operation exposes to bombing Belgium and Northern France friendly territories, the populations of which it would be tactless to alienate.

Churchill, who must have been in one of his good moods, writes to Eisenhower on the 3ᵈ of April :

— *The Cabinet considers with ansciousness and even hostility the project to bomb so many French Railway Centers owing to the fact that tens of thousands of civilians, men, women and children will be killed or wounded in the process. Owing to the fact that they are all friendly, this action might be considered exagerately rigorous and might create great hathred against the Allied Air Forces.*

Ike answers the 5ᵗʰ of April :

— *We must never forget that one of the fundamental elements which induced us to undertake Overlord, was the conviction that our overwhelming Mastery of the Air, made possible an operation, which could otherwise be considered, as extremely risky, not to say reckless... The arguments presented against the bombing of Communications Centers in occupied Countries are assuredly very strong. But my military advisors and I are convinced that this bombing will increase our chances of success in the difficult battle ahead... Personally, I believe the calculations of probable losses have been grossly exaggerated.*

SHAEF were then considering 80.000 probable victims, of which 20.000 killed amongst the French Population. Churchill, let matters be, perhaps was he only seeking an alibi for after war years. He leaves matters as they are and on the 7ᵗʰ of May, one month later he advises Roosevelt of his preoccupations :

— The War Cabinet is very perturbed since three weeks because of the number of French killed, during Air raids on the Railway Centers... However, three seventh of these raids have already been carried out, and results show that the losses in the civilian population are by far lower than those foreseen by the authorities... The Cabinet would appreciate your opinion.

— The U.S. President answers on the 11th of April :

— I fully share your anguish concerning the victims caused amongst the French Population... I am too, as you are, convinced that all possible precautions have been taken. However deplorable the losses in human lives may be I am not prepared to impose, from so far away, to the responsible chiefs, the slightest restriction in their action.

66.000 Tons of bombs are affected to « Transportation Plan ». The Tactical Air Force first of all blows up the bridges of the Albert Canal on the Meuse, then according to a line Antwerp, Liège, Namur; then those of the Seine from Le Havre to Paris; and finally those of the Loire from Blois to Nantes. Then from the month of May, inside this parallel, 80 targets are attacked, of which Charleroi, Courtrai, Hasselt, Gand, Liège and Louvain in Belgium; Boulogne, Lille, Metz, Mulhouse, Orléans, Reims, Tourcoing and Troyes in France.

The evaluating Services estimate that 51 Targets were totally destroyed, 25 suffered considerable damage, 4 were slightly damaged. It is certain this estimation is grossly exagerated : the major part of the main lines, which were destroyed, were repaired within a week. Notwithstanding, the landing zone is really cut off from the rest of Europe, and the eventual arrival of reserves, considerably hindered by the damage caused to public works. The 1st of June 1944, the rail trafic is reduced by half over the complete French territory.

The two Air Forces strategical and tactical took advantage of their numerous raids in order to engage in battle the German fighters. They either withdrew or suffered heavy losses (1) .

On D.Day, Marshal Sperrle and his 3d *Luftflotte* have at their disposal only 198 bombers and 125 fighters. Finally, in the few days before the landing, repeated bombings put out of action most of the heavy batteries along the North Coast of France.

---

(1) The Luftwaffe lost nearly 2500 units, 500 of which in Air Battles during the first 5 months of 1944.

During the first week of June, the Germans are on the alert from Boulogne to Brest.

5. The final plan

The initial Overlord plan, established by General Morgan and COSSAC, was found unsatisfactory by its first three readers : Eisenhower, Bedell-Smith, his chief of staff and Montgomery.
Three questions had to be asked :

— *Was not the front too narrow ?*
— *The landing zone too reduced ?*
— Could the problem of the ports be solved ?

Eisenhower discussed it with his two collaborators, the 31st of December 1943, in Marrakech, before his trip to the States, when Churchill, in convalescence, remitted to them a copy of the Plan.

Upon his return to London, on the 14th of January, he studies the proposals of Smith, Montgomery, Ramsay and Leigh-Mallory.

Certainly, COSSAC chose the landing zone by a procedure of elimination. Five possibilities were discarded, to the benefit of the Bayeux Sector, where the tide and the defenses present the most favourable aspects. But according to the advice of the experts, the initial plan should be altered. They propose modifications which Eisenhower adopts as from the 21st of January 1944 :

1. *D.Day will be put back, to the 1st to the 31st of May in order to allow a prospective preparation over 6 months, from D-90 (1 March) to D+90 (31 August)(1).*
2. *The landing Area will be widened from 40 to 80 kilometers.*
3. *The means will be increased, from 3 to 5 Divisions and two airborne Brigades of 3 Divisions, in the Assault wave.*

Admiral Ramsay is enthrusted with the misson of bringing all these forces to the predetermined pin-points; in the fixed time, with 5000 vessels instead of 4000 : It will be the Neptune operation. Afterwards, Montgomery obtained further dispositions, in particular :

— *In order to prevent congestion on the beaches, the British and U.S. landing zones will be distinct.*
— *As soon as possible the British and U.S. Forces, will each dispose of a port in good working order.*
— *Two Divisions will be sent with the least possible·delay to reinforce the landed troops.*

All the foregoing, of course, taking for granted that the Mastery of the Air will be achieved before the landing, by the Strategic Air Force, the tactical Air Force concentrating their efforts in helping the advance of the landed troops. Tedder and Leigh-Mallory agree.

---

(1) At the request of Ramsay, in order to gain a month's production for the Naval constructions.

*All is absolutely ready. Radar ↑ DCA
↑ ↑ Rocket batteries. → Fortress
artillery. ↓*

On the eve of D.Day the opponents their final work mettings.

(From left to right) Bradley, Ramsay, Tedder, Eisenhower, Montgomery, Leigh-Mallory, Bedell Smith. ↑ *Last inspection : Tedder, Eisenhower, Montgomery* → *Rommel, checked for the last time his deployment but he will be absent on D.Day.* → *The reception Committee : Admiral Kranke, General Speidel, G. von Schweppenburg, General Plocher* ↓ ↓
But the 6th of June at 0.00 hours General Maxwell Taylor buckles his parachute ↓ ↓ ↓ *The fate is sealed.*

The 6th of June, gone since midnight the first gliders are launched at 0.30 hours at the mouth of the River Orne with varied success.

In the preparation of these plans, Montgomery, real professional, plays the essential role. Eisenhower who never commanded but an infantry bataillon in the field, has neither the practical sense, nor the tactical imagination of his British colleague; he confines himself, with luck, to analysing the best ideas proposed to him.

Eisenhower's task is however complex : he must translate, into precise orders, the application plans and coordinate them in a constructive atmosphere. Human relations often prove to be difficult. The British establish detailed and minuted orders, leaving nothing to chance. The Americans are used to receiving general directives instead of detailed and rigid instructions. An American Admiral declares to Admiral Ramsay :

— *When I am requested to do something, I like to be told what to do, but not how to do it. That is my business !*

The General in Chief had also to see to the Secrecy of the Operation, a secret shared by more of less by tens of thousands of men. He took onto himself the desingation of reconnaissance and bombing raids, in order to lead the enemy astray, and maintain the effect of surprise, the majority of the Air raids took place over zones where the landing was not foreseen.

Eisenhower makes sure that all the drawers of the final plan fit properly, a harassing task, because he has to report to Marshall who has placed his confidence in him as well as to Churchill and Brooke who intervue in the details and seem eager to lead their own war. He is furthermore confronted with the assaults of the French, de Gaulle in particular, who, the 6th of June, substituted himself to Giraud, at the head of the French Forces, and cannot be held back.

Pleasant and conciliating, Eisenhower becomes charmer, but he applies his orders :

— *Not to give to the French any information, the disclosure of which, would be likely to jeopardize the success of Overlord.*

In April he advises the Russians of the approximate date of Overlord. Answer : The Red Army will launch an attack at that period. Without any other details.

The 9th of May having consulted all : the tide, the moon and meteorological experts, Ike fixes D.Day at Y+4. Y.Day is the 1st of June and from the 4th to the 7th the tides are favourable, furthermore, it is the full moon period.

At that date, many unknown factors still subsist for the Supreme Command :

— *No assurance that the enemy will not be rapidly able to bring mobile reserves to the landing zone.*
— *The zone in question is not perfectly isolated. Communications are only temporarily disrupted.*

18.000 parachutists jump at 0.50 hours.   This will be one of the first victims → →, whereas this other will be captured →

Notwithstanding, the Commander in Chief, disposes of another trump card : the French Resistance. He however hesitates to make use of it, as its reaction, once put into action, might well become uncontrolable. He will mobilize, at the last minute, only the Resistants of the landing zone.

General Koenig, Commander of the French Forces of the Interior (FFI) who protested against the deadly bombing of the civilian populations said to Eisenhower :

— *Indicate the Targets, we shall destroy them by sabotage.*

In order to reach the Seine and the Loire at D+9 SHAEF estimates that the following troops are required :

18 Divisions at D + 10
24 Divisions at D + 20
30 Divisions at D + 35

5 to 6 German Divisions will welcome the 8 Allied assault Divisions, as the experts estimate that with the arrival of reserves the Germans will dispose of :

12 Divisions at D + 10
30 Divisions at D + 20
37 Divisions at D + 35

The game will therefore be difficult to win. Churchill and Brooke are as pessimistic as possible and, until the last moment try to induce Eisenhower to delay the operation. Why not return to the peripheric strategy, attack in Italy and drive directly to Wien. Why risk the greatest disaster of the War.

With smiling scepticism Eisenhower wins his battle against the Prime Minister. He is prisoner of the mechanism which he has built up and all that he has to do is to see that it is well oiled.

Training is perfect, the morale of the crusade is excellent : all depends at present on the means of transport and on Admiral Ramsay.

On Y.day, Eisenhower anxious, interrogates the meteorology, Dr Staag, answer :

— *The situation is not what we expected. The evolution is slow in precising itself. Favourable on the whole, with respect to the wind, it is uncertain with respect to cloudiness.*

The first units start on their way, leaving from the North of England.

The evening of the 3d of June, Staag announces a strong wind for the period from the 4th to the 6th of June, low clouds and fog. In the afternoon, Churchill requests the authorisation of Admiral Ramsay to follow the landing operations. No, answers Eisenhower, should the vessel, carrying the Prime Minister, be damaged, it would immobilize four or five vessels who would fly to his rescue.

In other words, Churchill would be a supplementary worry in the battle. Ouf!

Those who come out of the gliders unhurt assemble their arms and supplies.

But the heavy material will arrive only in a few days.

On the 4th of June, the eve of D.Day Staag is again questioned.   Answer:

— *Nothing new !*

Eisenhower delays D.Day by 24 hours, the weather is too bad for the Air Force.

Monday the 5th of June, 4 a.m. situation unchanged, storm in the channel.   The question is crucial. D.Day on the 6th of June or postphone the operation to the 19th of June, at the end of a moonless night.   Staag foresees the wind weakening and the cloudiness becoming slightly less.

Eisenhower asks the opinion of his collaborators.   Smith is for the go-ahead, Monty also.   Tedder and Leigh-Mallory hesitate because of the low ceiling for the plancs.   Ramsay in any eventuality requests a rapid decision.

Ike listens, very tense, thinks a moment and concludes:

— *I am convinced that we are obliged to give the order.   I don't like it, but there it is.   We don't seem to have the choice.*

D.Day will be the 6th of June.   The officers retire to give the orders for departure.

Eisenhower will give a further important directive.   It means a supplementary precaution.   On the 4th of June General Gubbins of S.O.E. and his American assistant Col David Bruce of O.S.S. paid a visit to General Koenig to ask him if he saw any inconvenience in giving orders to the Resistance simultaneously to the whole of France and not only to the landing zone as had previously been agreed upon.   This in order to make more difficult the situation of the enemy.   Once more, there is the question of the civilian population who will be exposed.   Koenig agrees.

Eisenhower then starts the mechanism, the morning of the 5th, all the messages of uprising addressed to the French Resistance, go over on the BBC the same night.

The uprising takes place during the night. It will dislocate the German communications create an atmosphere of insecurity for the *Wehrmacht*, but also will cause atrocious dramas: Vercors, Tulle...

6. Operation Neptune

The 6th of June, at dawn, Admiral Ramsay bears the complete responsability of the conveyance of the Allied Divisions to Normandy.

His Plan, the Neptune operation, was meticulously studied at set. The alterations brought to the initial COSSAC plan, increased considerably the need for warships : 759 instead of 467. The widening of the front brought the SHAEF exigencies from 12 to 25 fleets of mine sweepers.

It was necessary to build or transform 80 types of landing craft.

In total the war fleet utilised for the landing will comprise 567 units of the Royal Navy and Canadian Navy; 175 of the US Navy; 11 of the Allied Navies.

Admiral King, preoccupied by the Pacific War, delivers his vessels parcimoniously : from the 1st of May 1944, he will have remitted to Ramsay less than 10 % of the landing craft which he is firmly holding on to. It is therefore for Britain, in less than five months, to build the required vessels.

To meet the wish of SHAEF, to dispose rapidly of two good ports, and in view of the probable hard defense of Cherbourg, the Churchill-Mountbatten project was achieved : two artificial ports, prefabricated, were built, which will have to be conveyed to the landing zone, docked and prepared to function.

The Navy had to be trained, the vessels had to be assembled at 10 different places, it was necessary to foresee and organise the embarking, to envisage the various possible incidents, on the trip, during the unloading; in short, not leave anything to chance.

That any man should be capable of taking on such a wager seems incredible; Admiral Ramsay, already the author of the Dunkirk Rescue operation, revealed himself, in this circumstance, an exceptional right man.

At 4 a.m. the bombing fleet takes off ↑
Here are the Hurricanes, → The Hali-
faxes who bomb the 15ᵗʰ German Army. ↓

This bomber Mitchell B 25
flies over the Orne River →

This Marauder bomber is on a vertical
above Utah-Beach ↑

I-D. Day

The 6th of June, at 2 a.m. two U.S. Airborne Divisions landed south of the Cotentin peninsula.   **The Ack and the wind disperses them.**   The losses amount to one seventh of the strength.   The Airborne do not succeed in isolating Cherbourg, but cut the road Cherbourg-Carentan.   The Germans are panic-stricken.

An hour earlier a British Airborne Division was released at the approaches to Caen.   Its task is capital, its consists in keeping the left flank, the most exposed, facing the *21st Panzer Division* of General von Feuchtinger.   The landing is also bad, and had it not been for the hesitations of the enemy, taken completely by surprise, the operations on the Eastern flank would have resulted in a catastrophe.

In the center between the two Airborne groups, serving as flank protectors, the landing Armada, 5.339 vessels appear on the horizon.   It is composed of two groups : The *Eastern Task Force*, under the command of Admiral Vian, carries the 2nd British Army under the command of General Dempsey, covered by the 2nd *Tactical Air Force* commanded by General Coningham; the *Western Task Force*, under the orders of Admiral Kirk, carries the 1st American Army commanded by General Bradley, covered by the 9th U.S. Air Force under the orders of General Brereton.

Since the previous evening mine sweepers clear the mines and mark out the ten access channels.   During this memorable day, the Air Force carries out 10.585 raids answering all intervention requests, and crushing all adverse Defense efforts.   The preparation of the field by the Naval Artillery and the Strategical Air Force, was such that, finally, the losses are low; the majority accidental.

Certainly, the landings on the St Laurent beach (*Omaha*) well defended, were carried out too far, as the first units came close to disaster.   At St. Martin (*Utah*), the situation was at times critical.

However, the evening of the 6th of June, in spite of raging seas, General Montgomery, chief of 21 Army Group, commander in Chief of the first phase, has at his disposal in Normandy 200.000 men, 10.000 of which only are out of battle.   It's a success, but the strategic Targets, fixed by the Plan, will not be reached.   One finds, furthermore a certain confusion in the forwarding of supplies.

What will Rommel do ?

Germain reaction

The Germans well informed concerning the intentions of the Allies, expect a landing on the French Coast. Admiral Canaris and the German Secret Services even had knowledge, since January, of the personal message :

The long sobs of the violins...

This signal over the BBC, was intended to announce the imminence of the operation. This message was correctly intercepted at Tourcoing, and interpreted by Lieutenant Colonel Meyer, intelligence officer of the 15th Army :

— *5th of June 1944 - 21,15 hours - Transmission of the second part of the message "Wound my heart with a monotonous languor".*

— *5th June 1944 - 21.20 hours - Therefore the landing will begin within 48 hours dating from the 6th of June at 0 hours.*

But since the 18th of February 1944, the German Secret Services, are in complete chaos : Himmler has succeeded in eliminating Canaris and in unifying to this profit all the Intelligence Services. The RSHA successor of the *Abwehr*, is in full reorganisation and proves itself incapable of exploiting Meyer's message.

The German Air Force has located the gathering of Troops and ships, in the South of England. The traditional reconnaissance planes have all been shot down, but 4 reactor planes, the first *ME 262*, succeeded in taking photogrphs of most of the British ports.

Hitler correctly analysed the situation. The 2nd of May, in view of the reports on the gathering of troops and ships in the West of England, he declared to his General Staff that the landing would take place in Normandy and ordered that the Sector be reinforced between the Seine and the Loire Rivers. It was more intuition than basic reasoning.

From his Headquarters at St.-Germain-en-Laye, Marshal von Rundstedt, Commander in Chief in the West, since January 1942, disposes of more or less one million and a half men, divided into two Army Groups : *Groupe G* and *Groupe B*, in fact 58 Divisions, at the date of the 6th June.

The Commander of Groupe G, von Blaskowitz, disposes of the 1st Army (*von der chevalerie*) stationed South of the Loire, and the 9th Army (*von Sodenstern*) placed opposite de Mediterranean, in total 14 Divisons, 4 of which are armoured.

The Commander of Group B (Rommel) was appointed to this post in January 1944. The Army Group B stretches itself from Holland to the Loire and comprises the 15th Army (*von Salmuth*), north of the Seine, and the 7th Army (*Dollman*) between the Seine and Loire, in total 44 Divisions, 4 of which are armoured. In fact 25 Divisions only are ready for

Sailing from the South of the Isle of Wight the landing Armada ↓ it anchored off the French Coast at 5.24 a.m. Dawn came at 5.30 a.m. The Navy began the shelling of the coast at 5.40 a.m; It's under this protection that the landing barges ← set off at 6 a.m. to reach the beaches at 6.30 a.m. ↓ . ↓ The sappers clear and mark out the channels through the mines and obstacles. ↑ The hardest is to begin.

combat, the others returning from Russia are at rest or being reorganised.

Runstedt estimates the landing will take place between Fécamp and Le Tréport, with the brunt of the assault north of the Somme.

Rommel, in charge of the strategic defense has the duty to face the onslaught, and thinks the operation will take place between the mouth of the Somme and St.-Malo, with a strong diversion action in Normandy. He is convinced, the enemy will attempt first to take the port.

On the defense procedure complete disagreement. Hitler insists upon a defense without the hint of retreat; on the *Atlantic Wall*, the fortified line, built at great cost since two years. Rundstedt feels that a fixed defense should be avoided, await the landing, and repel the assailants by a clever strategic manoeuvre. The marshal has at his disposal, for this purpose, the West Armoured Group (2 Armoured divisions, 12th Panzer SS and Panzer Lehr) under the orders of General Baron Geyr von Schweppenburg, who answers to him and not to Rommel.

Rommel's conviction is that the Allies will dispose of complete mastery of the Air. If they are allowed to land, it will be impossible to oppose waves of tanks covered by the Air Force. It is therefore essential to prevent at all cost, the landing, the battle is to be won or lost on the beaches. It is useless to count on reserves coming from the Rear, the only solution is to fight immediately with the existing means.

Rommel declares, end of April, that the enemy should be annihilated before reaching our principal battle field. We have to stop him in the water, and, not only delay him; we have to destroy all his equipment when still on board.

Upon his arrival in the West, Rommel inspected the beaches and gave orders to reinforce the **defence** by half a million diabolical traps and devices and 5 million mines to be laid in front and behind the Atlantic Wall(2). All had been foreseen and yet...

(2) Rommel had envisaged three Defense hypotheses: between Seine and Loire, between Somme and Seine, and North of the Somme should the landing occur in the South, Army Group C will withdraw to the Loire. In case of landings in the North and the South defense will take place on a line Seine-Yonne-Canal of Burgundy.

When the Allies land, during the night of the 5th/6th of June the reaction is the following :

St-Germain-en-Laye, General Staff OB West of Rundstedt.
6 June, 4 a.m., General Blumentritt, Rundstedt's Chief of Staff, advised of the landings of the Airborne, telephones to the General staff H.Q. operations direction, Berchtesgarden. General Warlimont is at the other end of the line.
— Parachutists have landed north of Caen and Carentan. Can we use the Armoured Reserves Panzer Lehr and 12th Panzer SS.

Through the marked up channels the men land from the barges,

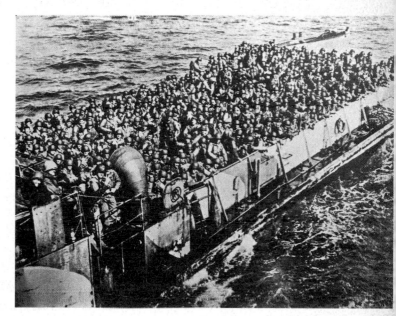

and have to reach firm ground one behind the other.

In fact we know Rundstedt was expecting a mass landing between Dieppe and Boulogne and he intended to launch against it the Panzers of Geyr.

In the morning, it is Speidel's turn to insist directly with Jodl to obtain the disposal of the 21st Panzer. Answer negative at 10 a.m. at Berchtesgaden, General Schmundt wakes the Führer. Admiral von Puttkamer announces the landing. Hitler convokes Keitel and Jodl. Upon the arrival of both officers, the Führer, very nervous, questions:

— *Well, it's the invasion? Yes or no?*

And he retires leaving the two men disconcerted.

At 10.15 a.m. Rommel still at home, listens to Speidel's report. He requests him to launch the automatic reaction foreseen for the 21st Panzer. The chief of staff can do nothing.

Speidel hesitates to take the initiatives which presumably his chief would have taken or obtained Hitler's authorisation. He keeps quiet, until the return of Rommel. In the course of the afternoon, he listens to an opera of Wagner, in order to remain master of his nerves...

At 12 noon precisely, Hitler, as each day holds his situation conference, at the castle of Klessheim, one hour's journey from Berchtesgaden.

Are present: Keitel, Jodl, chief of staff of the OKW, admiral von Puttkamer (for Doenitz), Goering (for the Luftwaffe), Schmund and a few auxiliaries.

The führer is overexcited. Jodl as usual, makes the general report. And Hitler again questions:

— *Is it the invasion?*

The officers, knowing well their remarks will be taken down in shorthand for the minutes of the meeting, speak as little as possible, measuring their words.

The führer is the supreme chief, he draws alone his conclusions:

— *Action must be taken immediately!*

Puttkamer and Goering promise an immediate reaction by the Navy and the Air Force. For the land Forces Hitler is victim of his own policy. Rundstedt has no freedom of action. Rommel is under Rundstedt's command but can refer directly to Hitler. Geyr obeys the orders of only Guderian, chief of the armoured troups. In effect no one has been able to act without the agreement of the führer.

The conference lasts three hours. After a long monologue, incoherent, interrupted by interjections and criticisms *ad hominem*, Hitler finally gives his awaited decision. Geyr's strategic reserve, the 12th Panzer SS and Panzer Lehr, will go into action. He further comments this order with great verbal energy.

View from the sky at 10 a.m. of the coast.

Progression is slow and the first wounded have to be helped.

At 16.55 hours Rundstedt finally receives from Jodl the awaited message :

— *The OKW wants the enemy Bridgehead destroyed, the 6th of June, before night, because of the risk of new support landings, by sea and by air. The beach must be cleaned to-night at the latest.*

— *Tomorrow, the 21st will counterattack with the "12th Panzer SS" and "Panzer Lehr".*

At 22.07 hours the sun goes down. One has to wait!

At the *Luftwaffe Headquarters*, preparations are made in order to keep the promises made by *Goering* at *Klessheim*. The *3. Luftflotte* under the orders of General *Sperrle* was helpless all day, what was the use of launching 198 bombers and 125 fighters against 5.112 bombers and 5.409 Allied fighters.

The 319 raids carried out the 6th of June by the *3. Luftflotte* all finished as a hecatomb. According to the chief of the German figther force, General Galland, the high command expected that the real landing would take place north of the Seine and wished to withhold air force reserves. Goering decided to throw in reserves during the day of the 7th.

From his headquarter in Paris, avenue du Maréchal-Maunoury, Doenitz gave orders all during the evening of the 6th.

— *Lay mines in front of all ports from Le Havre to Ostend, in order to hinder the awaited real landing.*

— *The motor torpedo boats of the ports situated North of Le Havre must attack the flank of the Allied Armada.*

— *The defense of the Ports must be reinforced to prevent at all cost the enemy taking them.*

At Portsmouth, alone, or nearly, Eisenhower reviews the day :

— *The landings were more successful than expected. All supplies were carried on to the beaches. The battle of Omaha was the only major difficulty. But on the evening of D-Day none of the fixed targets have been reached.*

During the day, Churchill rings in order to find out whether the allied troops are equipped with gaz-masks. He fears a German counter-attack with the use of gaz. Nothing confirmed those fears.

Rundstedt can't believe his ears. He gives orders to counter-attack the following day.

Blumentritt calls Speidel :

— The OKW is allowing us the use of the 12th Panzer SS and Panzer Lehr.

It is 17.00 hours, more than 12 hours have been lost. The two armoured divisions are immediately dispatched. The 12th SS, leaving from Lisieux will be on the spot the morning of the 7th. The *Panzer Lehr*, instruction unit, is proceeding from the Orleans — Chartres Area —

Ste-Mère-L'Eglise was the first French town to be freed before dawn.

53

ignoring all precautions, they start their journey during the day, are bombed by the strategic air force and suffer very heavy losses.

At 19.00 hours Rommel reaches Reims. He enters the *Kommandantur*, from where he calls Speidel.

— *What is the 21ˢᵗ Panzer doing! It must react!*

The chief of staff advises him he has transmitted Jodl's message to General Pemsel : *Throw back the ennemy before night!*

— *What did Pemsel say?*

— *It's impossible!*

— *If the 21ˢᵗ attacks in time, we shall repel them in three days.*

Rommel continues on his way, very anxious from the North of Caen, General von Feuchtinger and the 21ˢᵗ Panzer advance towards the Coast; but the British already solidly dug in, stop the tanks with bazookas. The 21ˢᵗ loses a quarter of its strength and does not attempt to go further.

A little after 21.00 hours Rommel reaches La Roche-Guyon. He dashes to the map : the counter-attack by the 21ˢᵗ has failed. The Marshal gives a few orders.

— *The 66ᵗʰ Panzer must remain in the Dieppe sector. A second landing in this zone is possible.*

II. THE BATTLE OF CAEN

It is not our intention to describe the Normandy battle. At the most, we can only draw the attention of our readers to the important decisions taken, in relation to that of the invasion. The perusal of the memoirs of the principal witnesses leaves the reader perplexed.

Should one be able to believe Marshall, Eisenhower and Montgomery, the impression dominates that the original plan took place pratically without a hitch : on D-Day + 90 the 6ᵗʰ of September 1944, the allies had, as foreseen, conquered the complete zone between Seine and Loire.

In fact, this conquest was effected in the face of an energetic defense by the enemy, and, without the trump cards which they held, the allies might not have been able to hold their ground.

In the first case, Eisenhower had taken everything into account except defeat :

— *We had nothing foreseen in case of failure, on D-Day, but, naturally, the Naval Commanders would have done the impossible to reembark the men. They would have covered the evacuation by fierce bombing. Should a disaster have occurred, they would have endeavoured to save all.*

In the second place, the two artificial ports, the importance of which was estimated to be vital, were taken across and finally secured, at the cost of great difficulties, on D-Day + 13. Immediately at dawn of this day the

Utah Beach was liberated at about 11 a.m.

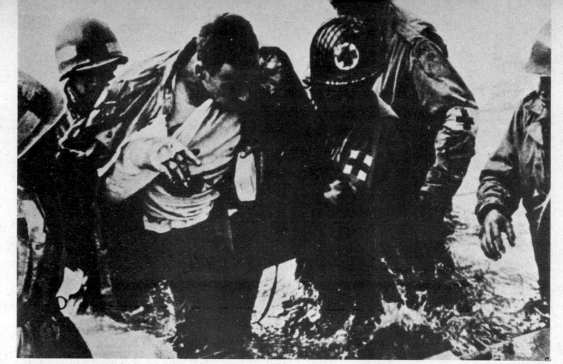

At Omaha Beach the situation for a long time remains confused. Amongst the sappers 11 men out of a total of 270 were killed or wounded whilst dismantiling explosive charges from the obstacles on the beach. The German batteries were not all distroyed and had to be shelled again. The first channel was opened only at 10 a.m.

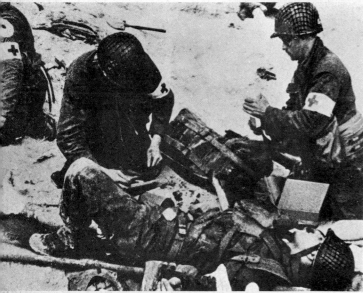

56

On the beaches reserved for the British (Gold, Juno and Sword), success was better in spite of the fact that the shelling, intended for the coast defenses, fell too far in the interior (inland). The British were equipped with ingenious devices to explode mines as they advanced. ↑
The glider men acted as excellent scouts. → The deployment of the tanks was rapid → A few of the captured mines and traps ↓ ↓

For these first German prisoners the war has come to an end.

Near Carentan, a civilian kneels by the body of an American killed in action ← *This British parachutist was captured by the Germans as early as the morning of the 6th of June* ↑

In the course of their advance the Allies overtake the bodies of their comrades ↑ ↑ *but also find the bodies of ennemy soldiers* →

wind started to blow with a force exceeding all expectations. The port allotted to the Americans (St Laurent) broke up and was put out of action. Furthermore numerous vessels were lost, on the first day, and this put in question the whole problem of supplies.

Ship losses in Normandy

	Destroyed by		Dammaged by	
From D to D + 6	34	64	106	106
From D + 7				
to D + 18	118	27	297	29
	152	91	403	135

A lull occurred at D + 18 and the Navy succeeded in making use of two small ports, Courseulles and Port-en-Bessin. Yet the daily arrivals of 220 to 230 vessels are reduced to 57 on D + 14; to 0 at D + 15, to 81 at D + 16 (22nd June). This of course upset the expectations, all the more so as 320 landing vessels (LCT) out of a total of 650 were out of action.

The artificial port of Arromanches functioned perfectly and, from the 10th of July, handled daily 6.000 Tons of supplies.

Arrivals of the allied divisions in Normandy

Dates	Forecasts	Actual arrivals
D-Day	5	5
From D to D + 5	13	12
From D + to D + 24	6	8
From D + 24 to D + 55	11	11
	35	36

The maintenance of the a/m pace is also a great achievement by Admiral Ramsay, particularly after the strong winds of D + 14 to D + 16. The conquest of Cherbourg at D + 20 the 26th of June puts an end to this period of insecurity. On D + 28, the 4th of July the Navy had landed one million men, 183.500 vehicles and 650.000 Tons of supplies. From now on it becomes impossible to throw the allies back into the sea. A pipeline under the channel (PLUTO) has been laid between Wight and Cherbourg supplying the Army, with vital fuel, without any transport means.

These Germans recuperated a British half-track and the British a Volkswagen!

*The pleasure of those Germans recuperating a Jeep ↑
and another one is → just visible.*

To the very last minute, isolated German snipers will fight with desperate energy → ↓
An artillery observator will be disloged from his church belfry ↓.

The front line fighters are now sacrificed. Some are dislodged from their blockhouses with flame throwers. Other wander aimlessly.

The happiest are captured and shipped to England.

The 6th of June at 2.40 a.m., here at the H.Q. of the 15th German Army, general von Salmuth was one of the first to be advised of the invasion. But at Berchtesgaden, they wish to think it is only a Diversion. Runstedt will receive only the 6th at 16.55 hours the order to destroy the Bridgehead before midnight.

Sub-lieutenant Ohmsen was the first man to announce the landing ↑ ↑
Twelve hours were lost.   The 12th Panzer SS Hitler Jugend (Lisieux) and the Panzer Lehr (Orléans) receive the order to proceed towards Arromanches.

On land, the armies under the command of Montgomery reach with delay, but exactly, their targets. This success is due in part to the errors committed by the enemy.

The delay of 12 hours in setting forth the armoured divisions was prjudicial to the enemy, but, would it have made a great difference, had the 21st division of Feuchtinger gone into action on the morning of the 6th of June ? No says Eisenhower :

— It serves no purpose to launch an armoured division if you don't know where you're going. It appeared to the enemy that we were effecting a small effort in the Cotentin Peninsula. But we had to gain Cherbourg, which was one of our main targets, because we needed a port to maintain the required supplies. At the same time we deployed important forces on our left, in the Caen area.

In fact, the effect of surprise played fully. The absence of Rommel on D-Day had no effect, but the interdiction to manoeuver without Hitler's authority paralysed Rundstedt, and later Rommel.

For the remainder, the allied mastery of the air decided on the fate of the arms on D-Day and the following week.

— From the start, relates Colonel von Tempelhof, chief of operations under Rommel, we were inferior in men and materiel. When it became evident that it was impossible to throw the allies back to the sea, the target of the German High Command was to maintain the front intact, and to delay as long as possible, the offensive in direction of Paris.

Night and day our troops were under the violent fire of the allied warships and artillery. The allied aeroplanes were masters of the sky, twenty four hours out of twenty four hours. It became impossible to move our reserves during the day. The fighter-bombers attacked all vehicles. The troops concentrations were hit by swarms of fighters and were decimated by carpet bombing.

And still the Germans were well equipped. Specialists maintain they had against the assailants superiority in heavy tanks, anti-tank artillery and bazookas (*Panzerfaust*). The allies will take thirty three days to effect the break-through, cleverly utilising their air force, their rapid tanks, their field artillery and their transport units. It appears however that the air force played the deciding role.

The German's secret weapon came into action too late. The first V1's are launched on the 13th of June; this weapon, still very inaccurate, has barely reached the experimental stage. The damage caused to the ports of Portsmouth and Southampton although appreciable, are without strategic value.

Another error, the German High Command has taken no precautions to make sure, under all circumstances, the crossing of natural obstacles, for example by tunnels under the Seine and the Loire. This lack of foresight, combined with the delaying action of the French Resistance, prevents the armoured divisions stationed in the South of France from reaching the front in time.

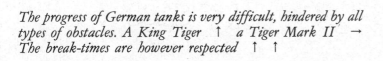

The progress of German tanks is very difficult, hindered by all
types of obstacles. A King Tiger ↑ a Tiger Mark II →
The break-times are however respected ↑ ↑

These reinforcements upkeep, boost the morale of the combattants who still hope to win and see coming to their rescue the spearheads of the Armoured units.

— Normandy was completely isolated, relates von Rundstedt. This delayed the concentration of reserves who took three to four times more than foreseen to reach the front line.

Finally, it took Hitler, Rundstedt, and Rommel two weeks to be convinced there would be no second landing north of the Seine. Two weeks during which the forces of northern France, Belgium and Holland remained idle.

In any case, Montgomery, who had correctly estimated the firing power of the enemy applies immediately the strategic conception which he succeeded in imposing.

— Tie down the German reserves in a hard battle of attrition, in order to permit the break-through of the front, on the other wing.

That was the battle of Caen.

With the help of the tactical air force and the artillery, Montgomery succeeded in compensating the local superiority of the *Panzerfaüste* and the armoured units. Rundstedt and Rommel wish to throw into battle the forces stationed north of the Seine, they confer with Hitler, the 17th of June, at Margival, near Soissons. Both Marshals would like to undo the locks, in time unbearable, of St Lo and Caen, in order ro regroup their divisions and set up a massive counter-attack. But the führer is adamant.

— You must stay where you are.

The two marshals in consequence have no freedom of action.

— As he wouldn't change his orders, relates Blumentritt, our troops were obliged to try to hold on to a tottered line. From then on there was no more defense. All that remained was a hopeless effort.

As soon as the Americans under Bradley took over Cherbourg, Montgomery orders Dempsey and the 2nd British Army to increase the pressure on Caen, in order to pin down as many ennemy divisions as possible. During the course of the battle, Bradley prepares a break-through towards St Lô, with the 1st American Army.

Finally, on the 7th of July, Montgomery calls in the strategic air force before Caen, and, after an intensive bombing enters the destroyed town. He maintains the pressure in direction of Falaise.

The 18th of July, a new aerial preparation smashes the German Resistance.

— In spite of three years spent on the Russian front, relates Feuchtinger, I never saw anything similar, as this day, 18th of July, will remain, for all those who experienced it, the most terrible day of the war. Two of my men committed suicide, another lost his mind. The combat resistance of all the others was weakened for a long time. This for the pshycological aspect. From the material point of view, the ground was rentered impracticable by enormous craters. All the tanks were covered by a thick layer of earth, some were completely buried. We were scatterbrained and distressed by the blasting. At midday we had one tank left in my company and five or

Danger comes from the skies, as the Allies have Mastery of the air.

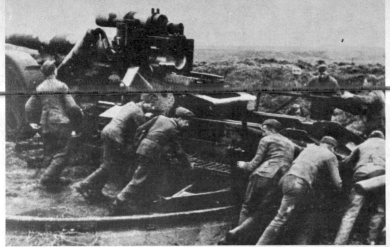

In spite of desperate efforts, the Germans lose ground hour after hour. the 319 raids carried out by the Germans (Luftwaffe) on the 6th of June resulted in disaster. On the Lesquin Aerodrome (the German Ace Joseph Priller 96 homologated Victories) admits his helplessness →

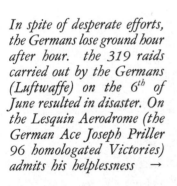

six in the battalion. 2.500 British and American bombers had taken part in the preparation of the operation.

At this date, the German high command was in complete reorganisation. The 2nd of July Rundstedt is recalled for health reasons, and replaced by von Kluge. The 17th of July Rommel, victim of a bombing raid, has been evacuated, seriously wounded. Geyr, wounded on the 8th of June, was sacked on the 5th of July.

At Margival, Rommel had already requested Hitler to put an end to the war and got the following answer :

— *Mind the landing front instead of interesting yourself in the pursuance of the war.*

The 29th of June, Rundstedt and Rommel called to Berchtesgaden, again ask the führer to put an end to the war. They are not listened to. Upon his return to Saint-German, Rundstedt has a telephone conversation with Keitel who asks him :

— *What shall we do ?*
— *Make peace, you fool ! what else can you do, concluded Rundstedt.*

The 2nd of July, the order of recall of the marshall as well as the führer's last directive arrived at Saint Germain :

— *All break through attempt must be stopped by dogged resistance on the field. Any shortening of the front is forbidden. No freedeom of operations.*

A few days later, the minister Speer visits Berchtesgaden and introduces to Hitler the chief of the fighter force of the West, general Galland.

— *My führer, Galland comes directly from the West front, he will be in a position to give ...*
— *I forbid you to intervene in the conduct of military operations, cuts in Hitler. Look after armements supplies, that's your job.*

He concludes, speaking to Galland :

— *See to the immediate execution of my orders. Gentlemen I havn't the time to hear any more from you.*

The 15th of July, two days before being put out of action, Rommel writes to Hitler a long descriptive letter of the situation and concludes by the following :

— *The troops are fighting heroically on the complete front, but the unequal struggle is reaching its end. I beseech you, to reach without delay the obvious conclusions.*

Marshall von Kluge is every bit as helpless. It is out of question drawing in the G Army Group as reinforcement, or of withdrawing the front to the Seine, as he had suggested. The break-through of the front

The most exposed are the civilians caught between two firing zones.

by the Americans will therefore be unequivocal brutal and irreparable. A weak German counter-attack in the region of Mortain, was crushed by the air force, whilst the troops of Patton and Bradley isolate Brittany, and, sweeping round, take the defenders of Falaise, from behind.

The 16th of August Kluge is sacked and replaced by Marshal Model. On his return journey he commits suicide by poisoning.

The Falaise pocket is reduced day after day, and, in spite of courageous counter-attacks; Model is forced to retreat north of the Seine, which the Americans reach the 20th of August.

The Germans have abandoned, behind them 300.000 men who, in order to hinder the allied supplies, still hold on to the ports of Saint Malo, Brest, Lorient, Saint Nazaire, La Pallice, La Rochelle and Royan.

Chester Wilmot is of the opinion that the landing could have been repulsed if the Germans had not been obliged to fight on a second front against the Russians.

And General Siegfried Westphal concludes in the same trend:

— Had all the battles been victorious we should still have lost the war ... The fundamental and fatal decision was Hitler's error to believe that the occidental nations would have allowed him to destroy Poland, without intervening. Germany is not capable of fighting on several fronts and winning the war.

The liberated towns are towns destroyed which have to be conquered ruin by ruin.

As soon as the liberators reach the suburbs they have to expect traps.

The 27th of June after Bradley had taken Cherbourg, Montgomery (↑ with Bradley and Dempsey) decides to increase the pressure on Caen in order to draw all the weight of the enemy. Victory will be achieved thanks to the Strategic Air Force and Churchill then comes to inspect the front.

The evening of the 6th of June 200.000 Allied soldiers have landed on Normandy, soil, 10.000 only are put out of combat. Such is the assessment which Eisenhower, exhausted but reassured, has been able to draw up.

PARIS
ROUEN
LE MANS
LAVAL

NDE PHARMAC
U PROGR

Even if the targets foreseen by the Allies have not been reached, Rommel back at his Headquarters of La Roche-Guyon, at 21.00 hours, is the great vanquished of the day.

There are no **exact** and complete statistics of the human losses.

It is, on the other hand, very irritating to note, that military historians practically never mention human losses : they follow the road to victory, without looking back.

■ The airborne losses, on D Day, amounted for the two American divisions to, 2.499 killed, wounded and lost, for the British division, 650 killed, wounded and lost.

■ On D Day, the allies landed 200.000 men, only 10.000 of which, were put out of action, including the a/m airborne losses.

■ On the 20th of August, the German army had lost in France 293.802 killed, wounded or lost and 200.000 prisoners; 1.529 tanks and 2.000 cannons were destroyed. The allies had lost, between the 5th of June and the 20th of August 209.672 men, 36.976 of which were killed. Their losses in tanks were superior to those of the Germans.

■ From the 7.300 V1's launched during the 80 days following the 13th of June, 17 % were shot down by the Ack., 24 % by fighter planes and 5 % by the barrage balloons.

■ The V1's which landed in England were responsible for 31.000 killed.

■ The number of French victims due to the allied air raids from 1941 to 1944 finally amounts to 50.450 killed and 71.159 wounded.

According to other sources there would have been 60.000 killed (National Institute of Statistics) or 67.078 killed and 75.560 wounded (R. Aron, **History of Vichy**, Paris 1954).

BIBLIOGRAPHY

This album is neither a strategic study nor a military or scientific reference document.

In order to situate in the general history this illustrated presentation of the Overlord operation, we should like to refer our readers to the following reference publications :

E. Bauer - **Histoire controversée de la Deuxième guerre mondiale.**
Rombaldi, Paris 1967, 7 tomes.

H. Bernard - **Guerre totale et guerre révolutionnaire.** III. Brepols.
Brussels 1966.

Sir Basil Liddell Hart - **History of Second World War.** Cassel.
Londres 1970 (éd. fse. Fayard)

J. de Launay - **Les grandes décisions de la 2è guerre mondiale**
(avec chronologie et statistiques). Rencontre. Lausanne
1975 - 3 tomes.

C. Wilmot - **The Struggle for Europe.** Collins. Londres 1952
(ed. fse. Fayard)

Amongst the **memoirs and souvenirs**, we note besides those of Bradley, Eisenhower, Montgomery and Speidel the studies and testimonies herafter :

K. Edwards - **L'Opération Neptune**. Jeune Parque. Paris 1946.
D. Howarth - **6 juin à l'aube**. P. Cité. Paris 1959.
R. Ryan - **Le jour le plus long**. Laffont. Paris. 1960.
P. Carell - **Ils arrivent**. Laffont. Paris. 1960.
D. Mason - **Breakout : drive to the Seine**. Ballatine. New York 1968.
R.W. Thompson - **D. Day**. Ballantine. New York 1968.
P. Jutras - **Sainte-Mère-Eglise et les opérations aéroportées**. Heimdal. Bayeux 1975.
R. Desquesnes - **Le mur de l'Atlantique en Normandie**. Heimdal. Bayeux 1976.

The Military Cemetries

Americans
Colleville-St-Laurent, on the coast between Arromanches and Grandchamp,
9.386 graves
Saint-James in the south of the department of Manche between Arromanches and Fougères,
4.460 graves

British
Bonneville-Sannerville, between Caen and Troarn,
2.175 graves
Bayeux,
3.934 graves
Brouay, between Caen and Bayeux,
377 graves
Cambes-en-Plaine, between Caen and Courseulles,
224 graves
Chouain (Jérusalem), between Bayeux and Tilly-sur-Seulles,
40 graves
Douvres-la-Délivrande, between Caen and Luc-sur-Mer,
927 graves
Fontenay-le-Pesnel, between Caen and Caumont-l'Eventé,
520 graves
Hermanville-sur-Mer, on the coast,
986 graves
Hottot-les-Bagues, between Caen and Caumont-l'Eventé,
965 graves
Ranville, near Pegasus Bridge,
2.151 graves
Ryes, between Bayeux and Arromanches,
630 graves
Saint-Manvieu, between Caen and Caumont-l'Eventé
2.186 graves
Secqueville-en-Bessin, between Caen and Bayeux,
117 graves
Tilly-sur-Seulles, between Caen and Balleroy,
1.224 graves
Saint-Charles-de-Percy, near Bény-Bocage,
744 graves
Saint-Désir-de-Lisieux, near Lisieux,
569 graves

Canadians
Bény-sur-Mer — Reviers, near Courseulles,
2.043 graves
Bretteville-sur-Laize — Cintheaux, between Caen and Falaise,
2.959 graves

Poles
Grainville-Langannerie, between Caen and Falaise,
650 graves

Germans
La Cambe, between Bayeux and Isigny,
21.160 graves
Champigny-St-André-de-l'Eure,
19.794 graves
Huisnes-sur-Mer, near Pontorson,
11.956 graves
Marigny-La-Chapelle-en-Juger, near de Saint-Lô,
11.169 graves
Orglandes, près de Valognes,
10.152 graves
Saint-Désir-de-Lisieux, near Lisieux,
3.735 graves

In total: 13.796 Americans ● 17.769 British
5.002 Canadians ● 650 Poles
77.966 Germans

are buried in the Military Cemeteries in Normandy.